The Chinese New Year

Joanna Troughton

CAMBRIDGE
UNIVERSITY PRESS

Long ago in China, there once lived
twelve animals. There was a rat,
an ox, a tiger, a rabbit, a dragon,
a snake, a horse, a ram, a monkey,
a rooster, a dog and a pig.

When the old year was coming to
an end, all the animals began to quarrel.
Each one wanted the New Year to be
named after it.

The animals made such a noise
that even the king heard the quarrel
from far away.

The king had a wise daughter.
She asked the animals why they
were quarrelling.

"I want to have the New Year named after me," said the tiger.

"So do I," said the rat.

"So do I," said the ox.

"So do I," said the rabbit.

"So do I," said the dragon.

"So do I," said the snake.

"So do I," said the horse.

"So do I," said the ram.

"So do I," said the monkey.

"So do I," said the rooster.

"And me," said the dog.

"Me too," said the pig.

The princess said, "You can have a
swimming race across this wide river.
The New Year will be named after
the winner."

The animals agreed. They all lined
up on the bank of the river. "Ready,
steady, go!" said the princess.

All the animals jumped into the
water, and began to swim to the
opposite bank.

Very soon the ox took the lead.
But he didn't see the sly rat who
climbed up his tail and onto
his back.

When the ox was near the bank,
the rat ran up the ox's head,
and jumped onto the grass.

"I am the winner!" said the rat.

"Well done," said the king.
"The New Year will be named
the Year of the Rat."

The princess felt sorry for the
other animals as, one by one,
they all finished the race.

"The next eleven years can be
named after the other animals,"
she said.

And so the order is, Rat, Ox, Tiger, Rabbit, Dragon, Snake, Horse, Ram, Monkey, Rooster, Dog and Pig.